SCIENCE CRACKERS

Awesome ASTRONOMY

Raman Prinja

QEB Publishing

Created for QEB Publishing by Tall Tree Ltd
www.talltreebooks.co.uk
Editors: Rob Colson and Jennifer Sanderson
Designers: Jonathan Vipond and Malcolm Parchment
Illustrations, activities: Lauren Taylor
Illustrations, cartoons: Bill Greenhead

Published in the United States by
QEB Publishing, Inc.
3 Wrigley, Suite A
Irvine, CA 92618

www.qed-publishing.co.uk

A CIP record for this book is available from the
Library of Congress.

ISBN 978 1 60992 040 1

Printed in the United States

Picture credits
(t=top, b=bottom, l=left, r=right, c=center, fc=front cover)
Corbis 27b Ed Darack Science Faction; **NASA** 5t, 7t, 6–7b, 8l, 12l, 13, 15b, 17b, 20–21, 21, 22,
23, 26–27, 27rc, 28, 29, 31; **Shutterstock** 5b Gary718, 7c Mau Horng, 7c G10ck, 7c Denis
Nata, 9c Elena Elisseeva, 9t Roman Krochuk, 12r beboy, 16–17 Stephen Girimont, 16
dundanim, 17 Dundanim, 20br kzww, 20bl creativedoxfoto; **SPL** 8c David Hardy

Note
Web site information is correct at time of going to press. However, the publishers
cannot accept liability for any information or links found on third-party web sites.

In preparation of this book, all due care has
been exercised with regard to the activities
and advice depicted. The publishers regret
that they can accept no liability for any loss
or injury sustained.

The practical activities in this book have
been checked for health and safety by
CLEAPPS, a UK organization that provides
practical support and advice on health
and safety in science and technology.

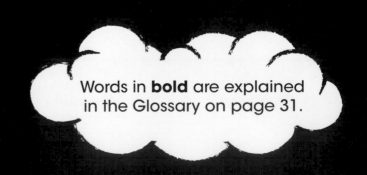

Words in **bold** are explained
in the Glossary on page 31.

CONTENTS

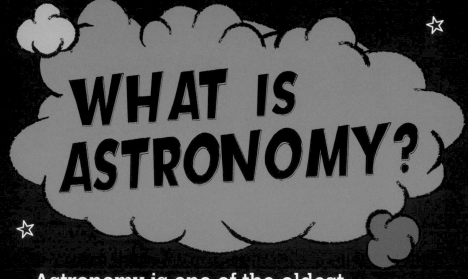

WHAT IS ASTRONOMY?

Astronomy is one of the oldest branches of science. It is the science of space beyond the Earth. Astronomy is the study of the **planets**, **moons**, stars, **galaxies**, and all the other objects in the **universe**.

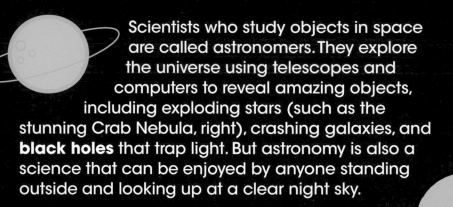

Scientists who study objects in space are called astronomers. They explore the universe using telescopes and computers to reveal amazing objects, including exploding stars (such as the stunning Crab Nebula, right), crashing galaxies, and **black holes** that trap light. But astronomy is also a science that can be enjoyed by anyone standing outside and looking up at a clear night sky.

HIGH TECH

Astronomers use powerful telescopes to look at the sky. Some of the telescopes are perched on mountain peaks, far away from the glare of streetlights and cities.

IMAGINE THIS...

Look up at the starry night and think of all the objects up there. Perhaps there are other forms of life somewhere. Will the stars always be there or will they fade away? Find answers to some of these questions in this book.

WAY BACK IN TIME

Astronomy has been of great importance ever since ancient times. The movements of the Sun, Moon, and stars were used to make calendars by the early Babylonian, Chinese, and Egyptian civilizations. Sailors of the past were guided across the seas by charting the stars. Many ancient monuments, such as Stonehenge in the UK (below), were built to represent the positions of objects in the sky.

ROCKS, GIANTS, AND DWARFS

The Earth belongs to a family or system of planets that all **orbit** the Sun. The Sun itself is a star, like many of the other faraway stars you can see on a clear night in the sky.

JUGGLING NINJAS!

In order away from the Sun, the planets are Mercury, Venus, Earth, Mars, Jupiter, Saturn, Uranus, and Neptune. To remember these names in the right order, try the sentence below:

"My Very Excited Monkey Juggled Seven Ugly Ninjas"

Use the first letter of each word for the right planet.

Our **solar system** is made up of the Sun, eight planets, many moons, and many dwarf planets. Lots of smaller bodies, such as **asteroids** and **comets**, also travel around the Sun.

Sun

Mercury

Venus

Earth

Mars

Light from the Sun takes eight minutes to reach the Earth

ROCKY WORLDS

The four closest planets to the Sun are rocky worlds. The Earth is the only planet with liquid water on its surface. This water has made life on Earth possible.

WHAT'S UP WITH PLUTO?

Pluto was once known as a planet, but it is now known as a dwarf planet. Astronomers think there may be more than 50 bodies in the solar system that are just like Pluto. These objects are different from the eight planets because they are very small and their paths around the Sun are not always clear of other bodies.

A FRUITY SOLAR SYSTEM

Imagine we made everything about a billion times smaller. The Earth and Venus would be the size of a grape, Jupiter a grapefruit, and Saturn an orange. Uranus and Neptune would be a pair of lemons.

Uranus

Neptune

Saturn

Jupiter

GAS GIANTS

Jupiter, Saturn, Uranus, and Neptune are known as gas giant planets. They are very large and mostly made of hydrogen and helium gas.

OUR STAR, THE SUN

DANGER!
DON'T EVER LOOK DIRECTLY AT THE SUN! IT CAN CAUSE PERMANENT EYE DAMAGE AND BLINDNESS.

The Sun is the largest body in the solar system. Almost 99 percent of all the mass of the solar system is contained in the Sun. The Sun is a huge, hot ball of glowing gases.

The Sun is really a small-sized star, and there are many similar stars in the night sky. The Sun looks much bigger and brighter from the Earth because it is much closer to us than the rest of the stars. The next nearest star to us, Proxima Centauri, is almost 270,000 times farther away. If the Sun were reduced to the size of a basketball and placed in London, Proxima Centauri would be a smaller ball somewhere in California.

Convective zone carries energy to the Sun's surface

Energy passes through radiative zone

MOODY SUN

The Sun goes through times when it is either steady or very active. This cycle in its behavior happens every 11 years. When the Sun is at its most active, many features can be seen on its surface. Sometimes there are dark spots known as sunspots. The Sun can also release huge amounts of gas and particles in an explosion known as a flare.

AURORAE

The Sun's flares send electrically charged material into the Earth's **atmosphere**, creating beautiful light shows near the North and South Poles. These are known as aurorae (or the northern and southern lights).

Core produces energy

SUPERPOWER

The Sun is made up of several different layers. Its incredible energy is produced in its center, or core. Here, a process called nuclear fusion takes place, and the gas hydrogen is turned into another element called helium. During this process, the Sun produces an enormous amount of energy. We can use some of this energy on the Earth using solar panels (below).

IMAGINE THIS...

You cannot visit the Sun. The main reason is that it is very hot. Even if you could get close, there is nowhere to land since it is a giant ball of burning gases!

PLANETS ON STRINGS

YOU WILL NEED:

- white cardstock
- compass
- ruler
- pencil
- scissors
- colored pencils
- string
- tape
- paper plate

The giant gas planets (Jupiter, Saturn, Uranus, and Neptune) are much larger than the four rocky planets (Mercury, Venus, Earth, and Mars). Make this solar system mobile and hang it up to see how the planets size up.

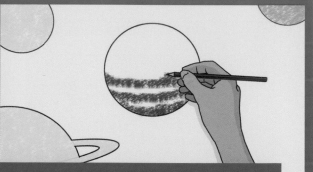

2 Color in both sides of the circles. Use gray for Mercury; yellow or orange for Venus; blue, white, green, and brown for Earth; reddish-orange for Mars; red or brown with white stripes for Jupiter; pale yellow for Saturn; light blue for Uranus; and blue for Neptune.

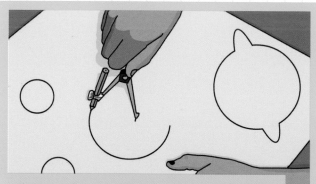

1 Using compasses, draw and cut out a circle for each of the eight planets from the white cardstock. Use the following diameters:

Mercury	¼ in (0.5 cm)
Venus	⅔ in (1.5 cm)
Earth	⅔ in (1.5 cm)
Mars	½ in (1 cm)
Jupiter	6½ in (17 cm)
Saturn	5½ in (14 cm)
Uranus	2¼ in (5.5 cm)
Neptune	2 in (5 cm)

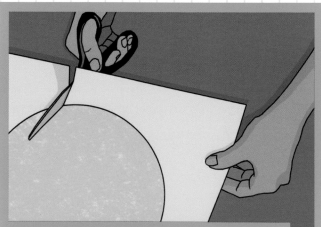

3 The Sun is too big to show on the same scale as the planets. Instead, draw and cut out a circle 8 in (20 cm) in diameter. Color it yellow on both sides.

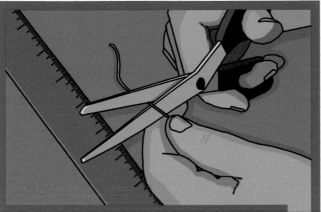

4 Each planet and the Sun will hang from the paper plate by string. Cut pieces of string the following lengths: 6 in (15 cm) for Mercury, Venus, Earth, and Mars; 8 in (20 cm) for the four giant planets; and 4 in (10 cm) for the Sun.

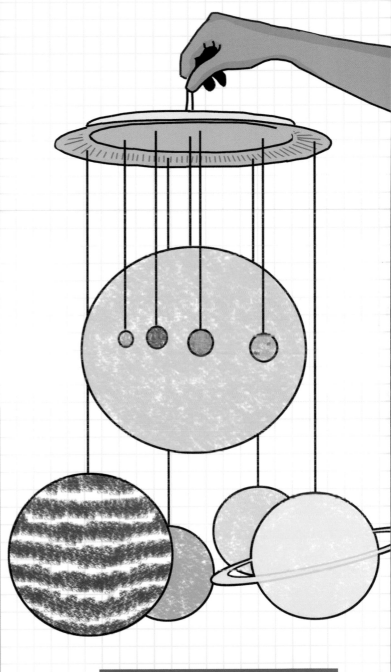

5 Attach each piece of string to the corresponding planet. Tape the strings to the plate. The Sun should be in the center with Mercury, Venus, Earth, and Mars forming an inner circle around it. The outer planets should be on a bigger circle close to the plate's edge.

6 Cut another piece of string and tape it to the middle of the other side of the plate. Make a loop on this string so that your solar system mobile can be hung up.

THE EARTH AND ITS MOON

the Moon is 239,000 miles (384,000 km) from the Earth

The Earth and its Moon make a very special pair in the solar system. Our home planet, the Earth, is the only one known to support life. The Moon is a very different place—cold and dry.

Our planet has an atmosphere of mainly nitrogen and oxygen gas, and liquid water on its surface, which make life possible. Our Moon is a cold, dry, and dead object. Its surface is covered in many **craters**, rocks, and a fine dark gray dust. There is no air to breathe on the Moon, nor is there water to drink.

ACTIVE
The Earth is one of the most active planets. There are regular earthquakes caused by movements of its crust and volcanic eruptions from beneath the crust.

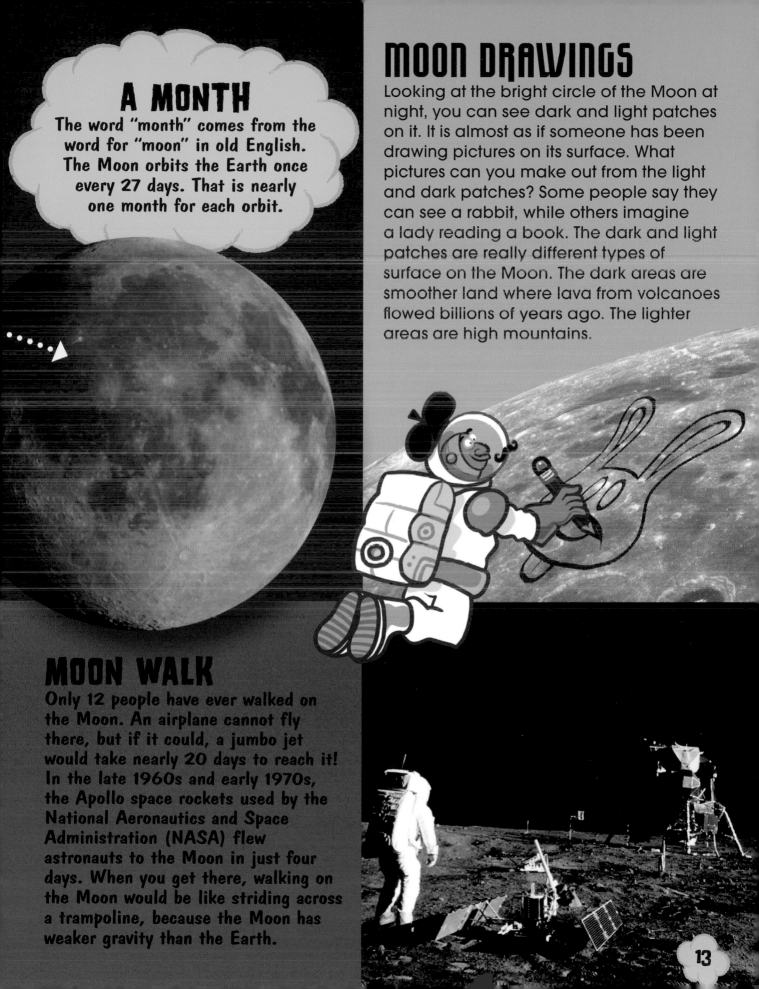

A MONTH

The word "month" comes from the word for "moon" in old English. The Moon orbits the Earth once every 27 days. That is nearly one month for each orbit.

MOON DRAWINGS

Looking at the bright circle of the Moon at night, you can see dark and light patches on it. It is almost as if someone has been drawing pictures on its surface. What pictures can you make out from the light and dark patches? Some people say they can see a rabbit, while others imagine a lady reading a book. The dark and light patches are really different types of surface on the Moon. The dark areas are smoother land where lava from volcanoes flowed billions of years ago. The lighter areas are high mountains.

MOON WALK

Only 12 people have ever walked on the Moon. An airplane cannot fly there, but if it could, a jumbo jet would take nearly 20 days to reach it! In the late 1960s and early 1970s, the Apollo space rockets used by the National Aeronautics and Space Administration (NASA) flew astronauts to the Moon in just four days. When you get there, walking on the Moon would be like striding across a trampoline, because the Moon has weaker gravity than the Earth.

CRATERS IN A TRAY

The surface of the Moon is marked by millions of craters. These craters vary in size from a few yards across to hundreds of miles in diameter. Most of the craters formed a long time ago when comets, asteroids, and **meteorites** crashed onto the Moon's surface. You can explore how different craters are made and how soil is dug up in this activity.

1 Fill the pan about ¾ in (2 cm) deep with flour. Lightly sprinkle the hot cocoa mix to cover the entire surface of the flour. The chocolate and white flour act as the upper soil and deeper layers of the Moon.

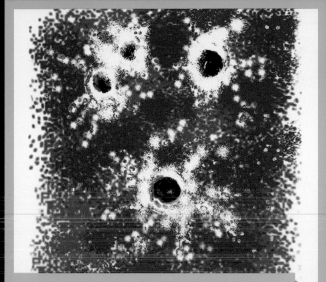

2 To make a model of the Moon's surface, drop (do not throw!) the marbles one at time into the pan. The marbles act as the crashing asteroids and comets.

3 Notice how the marbles make craters in the pan. The soil below the surface (flour) is brought to the surface. The Moon's biggest craters also reveal deeper layers of its crust.

Drop different sized marbles to see their impact. Drop marbles of the same size from different heights. Marbles dropped from the greatest height will make larger craters, because they have more energy.

WHAT'S IN A NAME?

Many of the Moon's craters have their own names. Some are named after scientists and artists including Albert Einstein, Leonardo da Vinci, and Alexander Fleming.

FULL MOON TO NO MOON

The shape of the Moon seems to change during the month. It is as though a giant monster keeps taking bites out of the Moon.

The Moon is not really changing its shape. What you see are the different parts of the Moon that are lit up by the light of the Sun falling on it. You see different parts of the Moon lit up depending on where the Moon is in its orbit around the Earth. The changing shapes are called the phases of the Moon.

27-DAY MOON CYCLE

3. First Quarter

4. Waxing Gibbous

5. Full Moon

6. Waning Gibbous

HARVEST MOON

An equinox is a time when day and night are equal in length. The full Moon closest to the autumn or fall equinox (usually around September 22 or 23) is called a harvest Moon. Traditionally this is when farmers brought in their crops before winter.

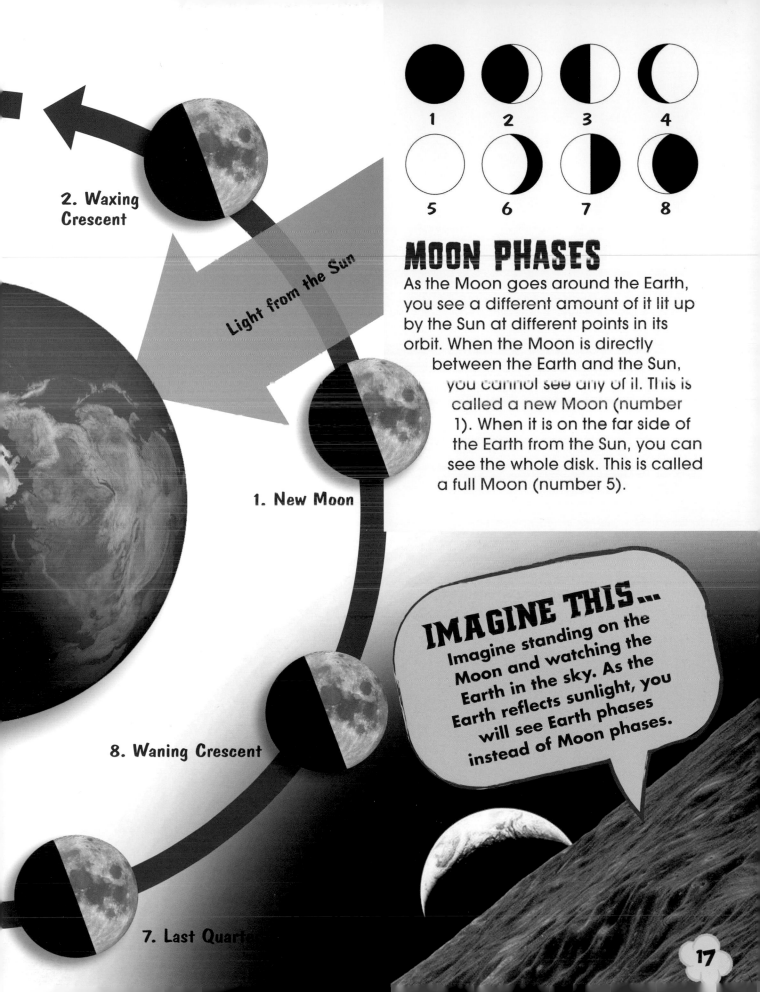

2. Waxing Crescent

Light from the Sun

1. New Moon

8. Waning Crescent

7. Last Quarter

MOON PHASES

As the Moon goes around the Earth, you see a different amount of it lit up by the Sun at different points in its orbit. When the Moon is directly between the Earth and the Sun, you cannot see any of it. This is called a new Moon (number 1). When it is on the far side of the Earth from the Sun, you can see the whole disk. This is called a full Moon (number 5).

IMAGINE THIS...

Imagine standing on the Moon and watching the Earth in the sky. As the Earth reflects sunlight, you will see Earth phases instead of Moon phases.

1   2   3   4

5   6   7   8

MOON FLIP BOOK

YOU WILL NEED:

- pencil
- thin tracing paper
- scissors
- glue
- 16 index cards 3 x 5 in (8 x 13 cm)
- wide tape

We have learned in this book that as the Moon circles the Earth, its shape appears to change slightly every night. This happens because different amounts of the sunlit part of the Moon are facing us on the Earth. In this activity, you can make a flip book of the Moon's different phases. These will cover the pattern of phases from new Moon to full Moon and back to new Moon.

1 Use the templates at the bottom of the page to trace the Moon's phases. Shade in the black regions. Make two copies of each phase.

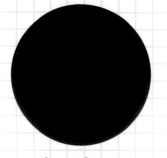

1. New Moon

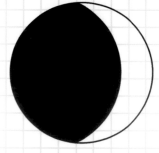

2. Waxing Crescent

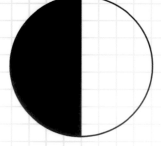

3. First Quarter

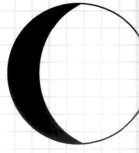

4. Waxing Gibbou

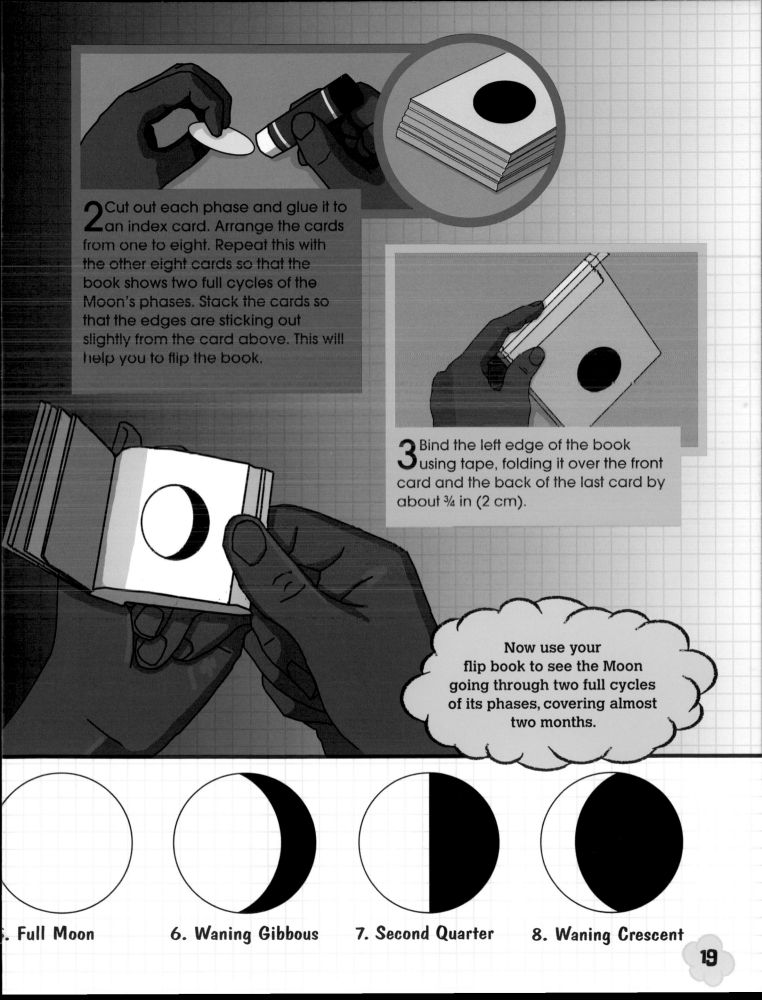

2 Cut out each phase and glue it to an index card. Arrange the cards from one to eight. Repeat this with the other eight cards so that the book shows two full cycles of the Moon's phases. Stack the cards so that the edges are sticking out slightly from the card above. This will help you to flip the book.

3 Bind the left edge of the book using tape, folding it over the front card and the back of the last card by about ¾ in (2 cm).

Now use your flip book to see the Moon going through two full cycles of its phases, covering almost two months.

. Full Moon   6. Waning Gibbous   7. Second Quarter   8. Waning Crescent

FROM DAY TO NIGHT

We all know that when the Sun is in the sky, it is daytime, and after the Sun sets, it gets dark. During the day, the Sun appears to move across the sky, rising in the east, and setting in the west.

But the Sun is not really moving around us! It appears to move because the Earth is spinning on its **axis** and taking us along with it. The time it takes for the Earth to rotate once fully is called a day. As it turns, people living on the part of the Earth facing the Sun experience day, and everyone on the part facing away from the Sun is in darkness. As the Earth continues to spin, the region of daylight moves across the globe from east to west.

MAKE YOUR DAY!

Use a globe to see how the spinning Earth leads to day and night. Mark where your city or country is on the globe with a sticker. Now shine the light of a flashlight onto the globe to act as sunlight. Slowly rotate the globe on its axis and see how the sticker moves into and out of the light from the flashlight, resulting in day and night. Note which countries are in darkness when it is daytime where you live.

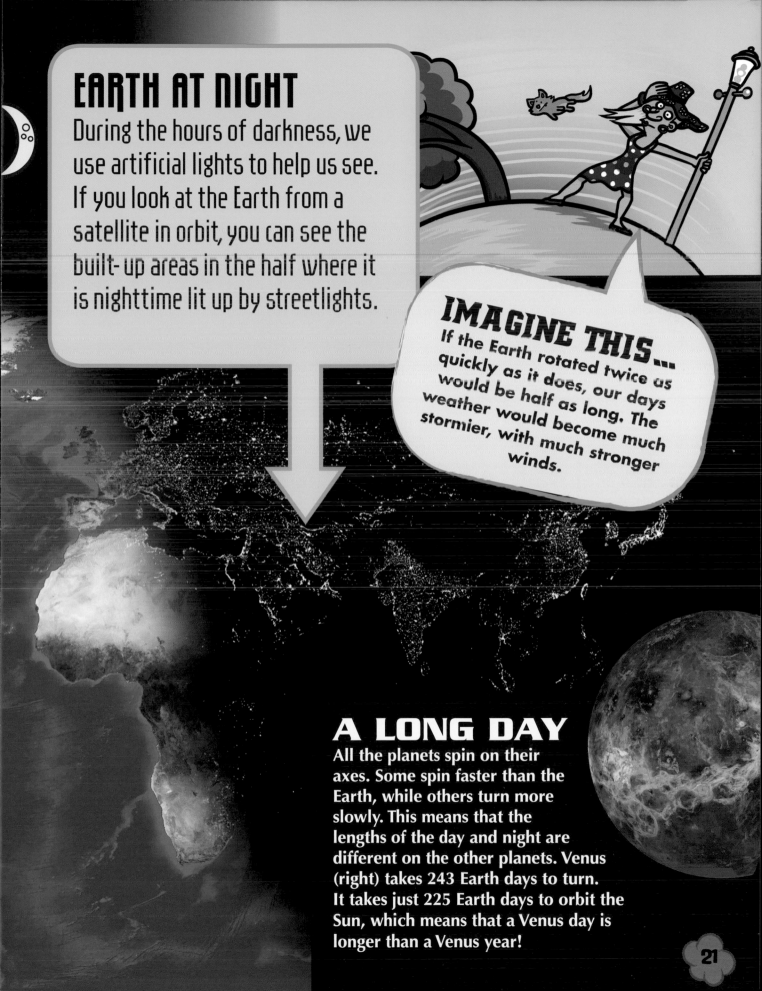

EARTH AT NIGHT

During the hours of darkness, we use artificial lights to help us see. If you look at the Earth from a satellite in orbit, you can see the built-up areas in the half where it is nighttime lit up by streetlights.

IMAGINE THIS...

If the Earth rotated twice as quickly as it does, our days would be half as long. The weather would become much stormier, with much stronger winds.

A LONG DAY

All the planets spin on their axes. Some spin faster than the Earth, while others turn more slowly. This means that the lengths of the day and night are different on the other planets. Venus (right) takes 243 Earth days to turn. It takes just 225 Earth days to orbit the Sun, which means that a Venus day is longer than a Venus year!

A ZOO OF STARS

Look up at the clear night sky from a dark location, far away from city streetlights, and you may be able to see thousands of stars.

Stars appear as tiny dots in the sky because they are so distant. Look carefully and you will see that stars are not all the same color. Most appear white, but some have an orange, reddish, or blue color. Stars are also not all the same brightness; some shine more brilliantly than others. The night sky is full of many different types of star.

STAR BIRTH

Stars do not stay the same forever. They have a birth, life, and death. All stars are born in clouds of dust and gas. Gradually, gravity pulls the dust and gas together, and at the center of the cloud, a future star, called a protostar, starts to form.

RED GIANT

Our Sun will last for 10 billion years. It is currently about halfway through its life. Toward the end of its life, it will expand to become a red giant. It will swallow up Mercury, and the Earth will become so hot that its oceans will boil. But do not worry, it will not happen for a very long time yet.

WHITE DWARF

After swelling into a red giant, the Sun will throw off its outer layers to leave the hot core, and a shell of gas known as a planetary nebula (such as the Eskimo Nebula, right). Over the next few billion years, the core will cool and fade to become a white dwarf.

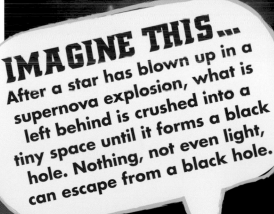

SUPERNOVA

Stars that are much heavier than the Sun have a more explosive end to their lives. These monster stars last only a few million years before they run out of energy to shine. The star dies in a spectacular explosion called a supernova.

IMAGINE THIS...

After a star has blown up in a supernova explosion, what is left behind is crushed into a tiny space until it forms a black hole. Nothing, not even light, can escape from a black hole.

CONSTELLATION IN YOUR HAND

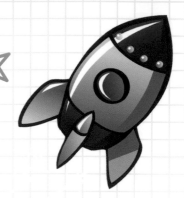

People have been looking at the night sky for thousands of years—even before telescopes were invented. Many have seen pictures or patterns in the way certain stars are grouped together. These pictures are called **constellations**. Here are six constellations that you can hold in your hand and look at. After you have tried this activity, see if you can find the real constellations in the night sky.

YOU WILL NEED:

- six cardboard tubes
- aluminum foil
- six labels
- pencil
- tracing paper
- scissors
- tape
- thumbtack

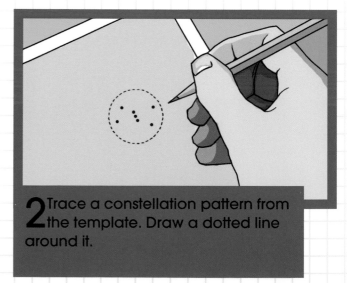

2 Trace a constellation pattern from the template. Draw a dotted line around it.

Orion

1 Take the cardboard tubes and cover one end with foil. Label each tube with a different constellation from the list on the right.

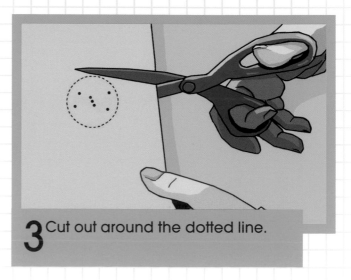

3 Cut out around the dotted line.

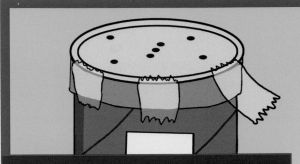

4 Place the pattern face-down on the foil on the tube with the matching label. You should still see the reversed pattern through the paper. Tape the pattern into place.

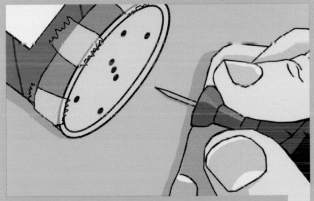

5 Using the thumbtack, punch a hole through the tracing paper and the foil for each star in the pattern.

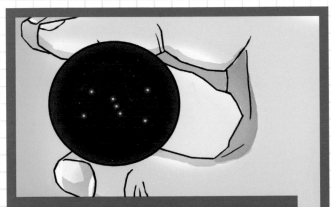

6 Remove the tracing paper. You should be able to hold the tube toward a light, look into the open end, and see the constellation as if you were looking into the night sky!

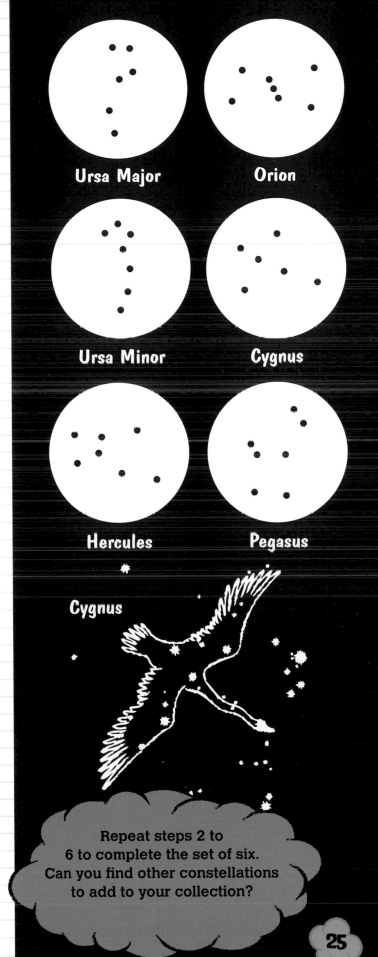

Ursa Major

Orion

Ursa Minor

Cygnus

Hercules

Pegasus

Cygnus

Repeat steps 2 to 6 to complete the set of six. Can you find other constellations to add to your collection?

NEW WORLDS FAR AWAY

One of the most amazing new discoveries in astronomy today is that our Sun is not the only star that has a system of planets orbiting it.

Using powerful telescopes on the Earth and in space, astronomers have so far found nearly 500 planets orbiting other stars far away. Planets going around other stars (and not the Sun) are called exoplanets.

IMAGINE THIS...

Maybe an exoplanet could have blue seas and white clouds. Or perhaps it has black plants. Maybe it has two moons. Draw some pictures showing how an exoplanet might look.

GOLDILOCKS PLANETS

The recent discovery of exoplanets has led to a hunt for rocky planets like the Earth that have living things on them. Think how fantastic it would be to know for sure that there was life, maybe like humans, on another planet very far away. Astronomers are looking for exoplanets that are the right distance from their star. Just like Goldilocks's porridge, the planet must not be too hot or too cold! It has to be just the right temperature so that oceans can exist on its surface. The presence of liquid water on a planet makes it more able to support life.

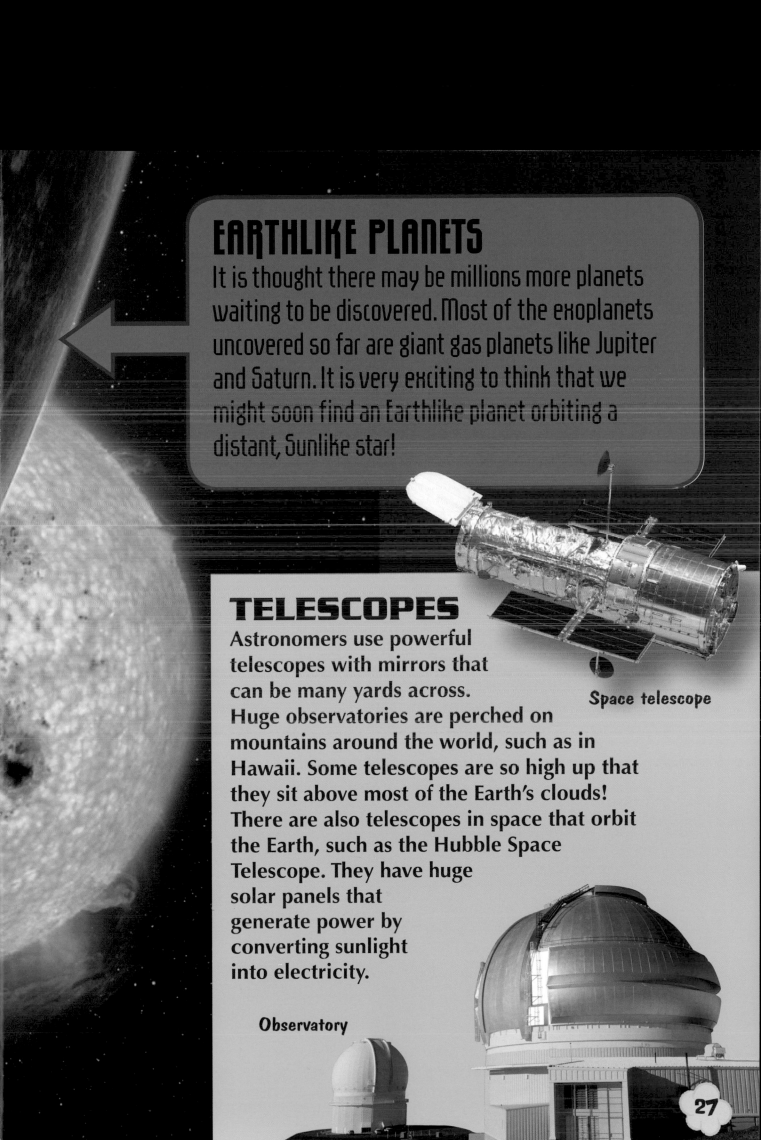

EARTHLIKE PLANETS

It is thought there may be millions more planets waiting to be discovered. Most of the exoplanets uncovered so far are giant gas planets like Jupiter and Saturn. It is very exciting to think that we might soon find an Earthlike planet orbiting a distant, Sunlike star!

Space telescope

TELESCOPES

Astronomers use powerful telescopes with mirrors that can be many yards across. Huge observatories are perched on mountains around the world, such as in Hawaii. Some telescopes are so high up that they sit above most of the Earth's clouds! There are also telescopes in space that orbit the Earth, such as the Hubble Space Telescope. They have huge solar panels that generate power by converting sunlight into electricity.

Observatory

A UNIVERSE OF GALAXIES

SPIRAL-SHAPED

The bright stars in our galaxy, the Milky Way, make a spiral-shaped structure, like a large, rotating pinwheel, in space. The galaxy is so large that light takes almost 100,000 years to travel from one side to the other.

Our Sun and its planets are just tiny specks among the 100 billion other stars that are held together by gravity to make our galaxy, which is called the Milky Way.

The universe itself is vast and contains all of the matter and energy we know of. The universe contains about 100 billion galaxies, which come in a variety of shapes and sizes. Our galaxy is a spiral galaxy.

A BIG BANG!

Astronomers believe that the universe began almost 14 billion years ago. They call the moment when the universe started the **big bang**. At first, the universe was an incredibly hot and tiny bubble. The energy released from the big bang made the universe grow. It might continue to expand forever, or it could stop growing and start to shrink back down into a tiny bubble.

10,000,000,000,000,000,000,000

ELLIPTICAL

These egg-shaped galaxies may have 1 trillion stars in them. While spiral galaxies have lots of old and new stars, elliptical galaxies have mostly old stars.

LENTICULAR

Between spiral galaxies and elliptical galaxies are the disk-shaped lenticular galaxies. Like ellipticals, they contain mainly very old stars.

IRREGULAR

Sometimes, a galaxy has no regular shape, perhaps because it crashed into another galaxy. Irregular galaxies have lots of new stars in them.

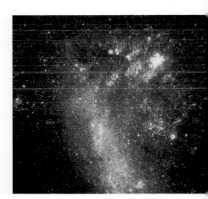

IMAGINE THIS...

Look up at the night sky and imagine how many stars there are. There are as many stars in the universe as there are grains of sand on all the Earth's beaches.

COLLIDING

Sometimes we can see two spiral galaxies colliding with each other. In time, these two colliding galaxies will combine to form one irregular galaxy.

PAPER COMET

Comets are balls of snow, ice, dust, and rock. Sometimes a comet comes close to the Sun. It partially melts and a spectacular tail streams out behind it. Follow these steps to make a paper comet.

YOU WILL NEED:

- scissors
- letter size sheet of paper
- paper ribbons
- tape
- drinking straw
- hairdryer

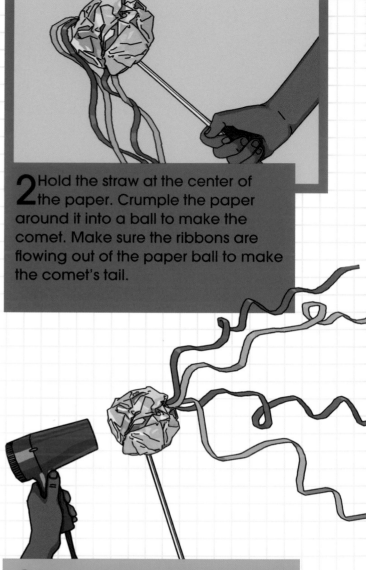

2 Hold the straw at the center of the paper. Crumple the paper around it into a ball to make the comet. Make sure the ribbons are flowing out of the paper ball to make the comet's tail.

3 Ask an adult to plug in the hairdryer. Blow air onto your comet to make the tails stream away. The air from the dryer is acting like the solar wind that flows from the Sun.

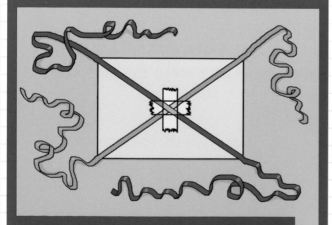

1 Lay down two ribbons across the sheet of paper to make an "X" shape. The ribbons should stretch at least a yard away from each corner. Put tape across the "X" where the ribbons cross.

Walk around the Sun (hairdryer) holding the comet, making sure the air is pointing at the comet. Notice how the tails always point away from the Sun.

GLOSSARY

ASTEROID
A medium-sized rocky object that orbits the Sun.

ATMOSPHERE
The layer of gases that surrounds a planet or moon.

AXIS
An imaginary line around which a planet or moon spins.

BIG BANG
The idea that the universe began with an explosive event.

BLACK HOLE
A region of space with such strong gravitational pull that nothing can escape it.

COMET
A small, icy object made of gas and dust that orbits the Sun.

CONSTELLATION
A pattern formed by groups of stars.

CRATER
A bowl-shaped hole made on planets or moons by objects crashing from space.

GALAXY
A collection of billions of stars, gas, and dust held together by gravity.

GRAVITY
A pulling force that attracts objects to each other.

METEORITE
A rocklike object that lands on the Earth or on the Earth's Moon.

MOON
A small object that moves around a planet.

ORBIT
To move around an object in a specific path. It can also mean the path itself.

PLANET
A large, round object that moves around a star.

SOLAR SYSTEM
The eight planets, many dwarf planets, and other objects that orbit the Sun.

UNIVERSE
All of space, matter, and energy, including all planets, stars, and galaxies.

INDEX

FURTHER INFORMATION

http://www.nasa.gov
The website for NASA, with
information about astronomical
objects and space missions.

http://www.kidsastronomy.com
Games, links and information on
planets, stars and galaxies.